WHATEVER HAPPENED TO...

THE ROMANS?

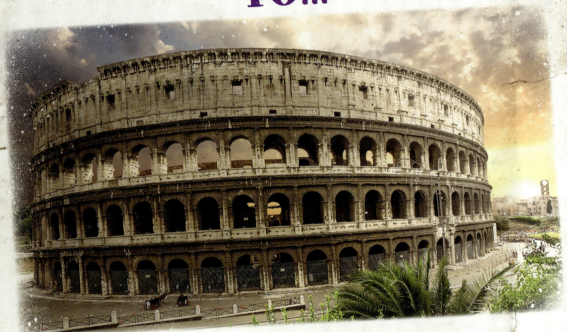

BY KIRSTY HOLMES

BookLife PUBLISHING

©2019
BookLife Publishing Ltd.
King's Lynn
Norfolk, PE30 4LS

All rights reserved.
Printed in Malaysia.

A catalogue record for this book is available from the British Library.

ISBN: 978-1-78637-884-2

Written by:
Kirsty Holmes

Edited by:
John Wood

Designed by:
Dan Scase

All facts, statistics, web addresses and URLs in this book were verified as valid and accurate at time of writing.

No responsibility for any changes to external websites or references can be accepted by either the author or publisher.

BC AND AD

In this book, you will see **BC** after and **AD** before some dates. And some of the dates might look backwards. What's going on?

AD stands for **Anno Domini** and that means 'in the year of the Lord'. Christian calendars count forwards from the year they believe Jesus Christ was born. When you see AD, you are counting forwards on the timeline.
AD 1750 = 1750 years after Jesus was born.

BC stands for **Before Christ**. If you see this next to a date, it means this happened before the birth of Jesus Christ. When you see BC, you are counting backwards on the timeline.
1750 BC = 1750 years before Jesus was born.

When describing a range of dates, you always count forwards.
So "between 1500 and 500 BC" or "from AD 500 to AD 1500" is correct.

Check back here if you need to.

JESUS

2000 BC   1500 BC   1000 BC   500 BC

WRITE THE YEAR AND THEN BC

CONTENTS

WORDS THAT LOOK LIKE <u>THIS</u> ARE EXPLAINED IN THE GLOSSARY ON PAGES 30 AND 31.

BORN

AD 500   AD 1000   AD 1500   AD 2000

WRITE AD AND THEN THE YEAR

WHATEVER HAPPENED TO THE ANCIENT ROMANS?

GLADIATORS, ET CETERA...

Imagine ancient Rome. I bet you're imagining bronzed gladiators training in the arena. Maybe you're thinking of rows of **LEGIONARIES**, with armour gleaming in the sunlight? Or perhaps you are thinking of Mars, god of war, or Jupiter, ruler of the skies? Yep – you certainly know who the ancient Romans were! Clever you. But have you ever wondered where they went?

Where did the **CULTURE**, people and traditions of one of the world's most **ICONIC** civilisations go?

IN ANCIENT POMPEII, PART OF THE ANCIENT ROMAN WORLD, PEOPLE WROTE ON THE WALLS THEIR THOUGHTS ABOUT LIFE. THIS IS GRAFFITI.

TODAY, IN VERONA, ITALY, PEOPLE WRITE MESSAGES OF LOVE ON THE WALLS.

OH NO! SOMEONE'S DRAWN ALL OVER THIS OLD BIT OF WALL! DON'T WORRY. I'LL HAVE THAT CLEAN IN A JIFFY!

STOP! THAT'S PRICELESS ROMAN GRAFFITI!

4

WHERE DID EVERYBODY GO? WAS IT SOMETHING I SAID?

OUT WITH THE OLD AND IN WITH THE NEW

It's easy to forget that ancient peoples were just like us in many ways. They had families, jobs, homes and leaders, just like we do. But life as they knew it then was very different to life as we know it now. I bet you haven't ever eaten roasted dormouse, and I wonder what the Romans would think of our microwave dinners! In this book, we will take a look at how the world of ancient Rome ended, and where all those things might have gone...

WAIT, WHAT?
TRANSLATE FROM LATIN HERE:

ET CETERA = AND SO FORTH

TURN THE PAGES OF HISTORY!

WHO WERE THE ANCIENT ROMANS?

WHERE ON EARTH?

The Roman Empire was, well, MASSIVE....

Rome

THE ROMAN EMPIRE in its greatest extent. Scale of Miles.

WHY DO LEGIONARIES ALWAYS HAVE SORE FEET? BECAUSE THEY'RE ALWAYS ROMAN AROUND!

I JUST HOPE YOU ARE BETTER AT FIGHTING THAN TELLING JOKES...

LEGIONARIES

GENERALS

GLADIATORS

OK, LADS. THAT WAS A GREAT DAY OF TRAINING. WHO'S UP FOR A BATH?

ROMAN BATHS WERE USED FOR BATHING AND MEETING OTHER ROMANS. THESE BATHS ARE IN A TOWN CALLED BATH IN THE UK.

OH, GODS!

The Romans believed in lots of gods who were each in charge of different things. For example, Jupiter was the leader of the Roman gods. He had control of the sky and lightning.

THUNDERBOLTS AND LIGHTNING. VERY, VERY FRIGHTENING...

THE FAMILIA

The oldest male in a family was in charge, and he was known as the paterfamilias. The paterfamilias was usually the only person who could own property or make decisions. The paterfamilias decided who got to join a familia through **ADOPTION**. Everyone else in the familia belonged to the paterfamilias as if they were property, and he got to decide everything about their lives – including being able to put them to death if he wished.

Paterfamilias
The head of the familia

Materfamilias
The wife of the paterfamilias

Sons
By birth or adoption, sons can start their own families on marriage or stay in the familia

Daughters
The paterfamilias usually decides who daughters marry. Leave upon marriage to join their new husband's family

DAUGHTERS-IN-LAW
Upon marriage they become part of this familia

Grandchildren
May be part of their father's family or remain under control of the paterfamilias

Freedmen
Freed slaves who were loyal to the familia but were free to start their own familia

Skilled slaves
Skilled or educated slaves could hope to become freed

Unskilled slaves
Had no power

WAIT, WHAT?
TO PRONOUNCE THIS WORD, SAY:
PATERFAMILIAS = PAY-TER-FAM-ILLY-AS

7

PAX ROMANA

TIME TO CHILL OUT

From the **REIGN** of Augustus (27 BC to AD 14) to the end of the time of Marcus Aurelius (AD 161 to AD 180), the Roman world was, more or less, at peace. This was called the Pax Romana – pax means peace in Latin. The Roman Empire protected each **PROVINCE** and the provinces were allowed to make their own laws, as long as they accepted being controlled by Rome.

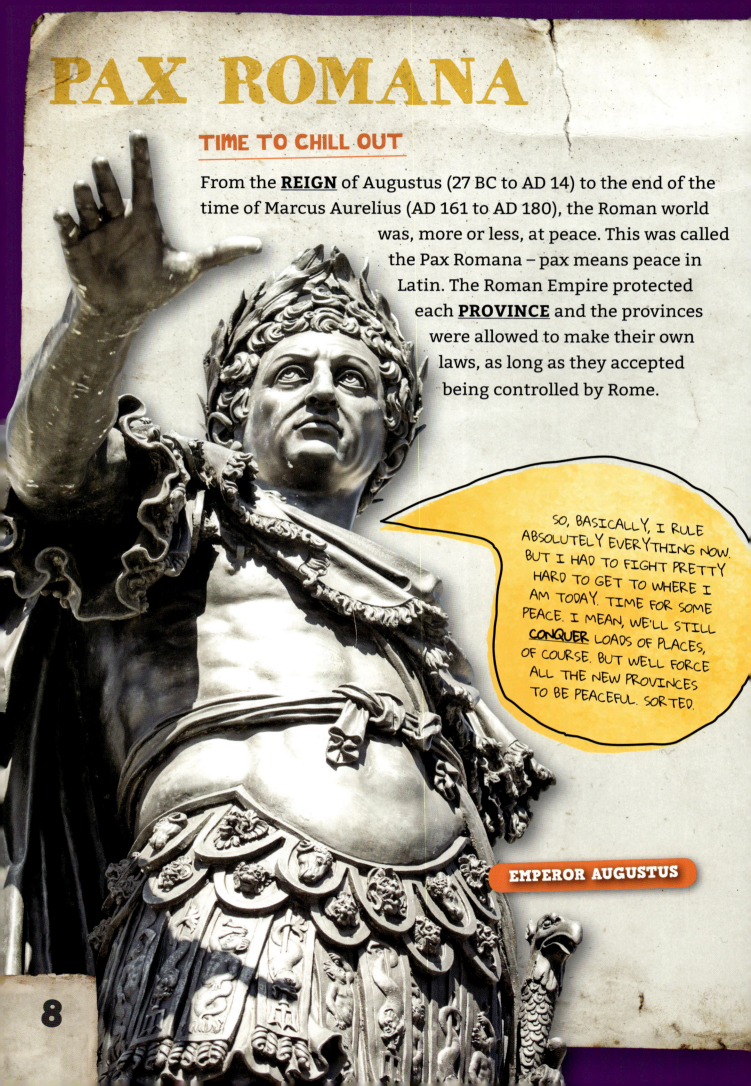

SO, BASICALLY, I RULE ABSOLUTELY EVERYTHING NOW. BUT I HAD TO FIGHT PRETTY HARD TO GET TO WHERE I AM TODAY. TIME FOR SOME PEACE. I MEAN, WE'LL STILL **CONQUER** LOADS OF PLACES, OF COURSE. BUT WE'LL FORCE ALL THE NEW PROVINCES TO BE PEACEFUL. SORTED.

EMPEROR AUGUSTUS

THESE ARE GOOD TIMES TO BE A FARMER IN ANCIENT ROME.

I FOUND ROME A CITY OF BRICK, AND LEFT IT ONE OF MARBLE. PAT ON THE BACK FOR ME... NOW COULD SOMEONE GET THIS BABY OFF MY LEG, PLEASE?

GOLD STAR FOR AUGUSTUS

Augustus did a great job of running Rome itself. He made sure everyone would be OK if there was a fire or a flood, and made sure there wouldn't be <u>FAMINES</u> for the people of Rome. He took charge of the water, roads and food, made the police force bigger and rebuilt temples. The next few emperors kept the peace going. Pax Romana would last almost 200 years.

WAIT, WHAT?
TO PRONOUNCE THESE WORDS, SAY:

AUGUSTUS = OR-GUS-TUSS

MARCUS AURELIUS = MAR-CUSS OR-AY-LEE-US

EMPERORS BEHAVING BADLY

THE TROUBLE WITH EMPERORS

The emperors of Rome could be good, and they could be bad. The trouble with emperors was that they had absolute power – this meant they could do whatever they wanted. This sounds great, but the type of person who might have wanted that kind of power might not have been the kind of person you would have wanted to be emperor...

I'M EMPEROR CALIGULA. PEOPLE MIGHT HAVE THOUGHT IT WAS A GOOD IDEA WHEN I BECAME EMPEROR, BUT I SOON SHOWED THEM! HA HA HA HA! I'M ABSOLUTELY BONKERS! NOW I'VE DECIDED I AM A GOD! ALSO, MY HORSE IS A CONSUL NOW! WOO-HOO!

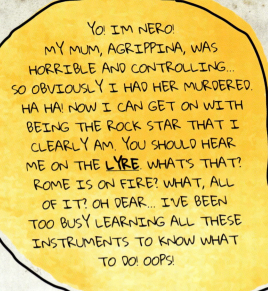

YO! I'M NERO! MY MUM, AGRIPPINA, WAS HORRIBLE AND CONTROLLING... SO OBVIOUSLY I HAD HER MURDERED. HA HA! NOW I CAN GET ON WITH BEING THE ROCK STAR THAT I CLEARLY AM. YOU SHOULD HEAR ME ON THE **LYRE**. WHAT'S THAT? ROME IS ON FIRE? WHAT, ALL OF IT? OH DEAR... I'VE BEEN TOO BUSY LEARNING ALL THESE INSTRUMENTS TO KNOW WHAT TO DO! OOPS!

MY NAME IS DOMITIAN. I'M NOT LIKE A NORMAL EMPEROR - I'M A FUN EMPEROR. I LIKE SPORTS AND GAMES AND FUN AND I ESPECIALLY LIKE CHARIOTS! BUT... I'M PRETTY SURE EVERYONE IS TRYING TO KILL ME. I MEAN, WHY WOULDN'T THEY? MAYBE EVEN MY WIFE IS TRYING TO KILL ME. AARGH! THEY'RE ALL OUT TO GET ME! SEND OUT THE SPIES!

WAIT, WHAT?
TO PRONOUNCE THESE WORDS, SAY:

CALIGULA = CAL-IG-UE-LA
NERO = NEAR-OA
DOMITIAN = DOM-ISH-UN

Did these party animals cause the end of the Roman Empire? We're going to look at the story of the slow fall of one of humanity's greatest-ever civilisations. It's a great story. And at the end, you can make up your own mind, young historian: whatever happened to the ancient Romans?

THE FIVE GOOD EMPERORS

AD 96 to AD 180

The high point of the Roman Empire was when it was ruled over by five emperors who were very different from the party-loving, strange emperors before them. These emperors were not related by birth. Instead, each emperor chose someone who would be the next emperor, and then adopted him. The first of this line was Nerva, a **POLITICIAN**, who took over after Domitian was **ASSASSINATED**.

Nerva adopted Trajan, who became emperor in AD 98. Trajan had been ruling in Upper Germany, and was a great general. He treated the senate with respect, looked after the people, and may even have given money to poor children in the Italian cities.

EMPEROR TRAJAN

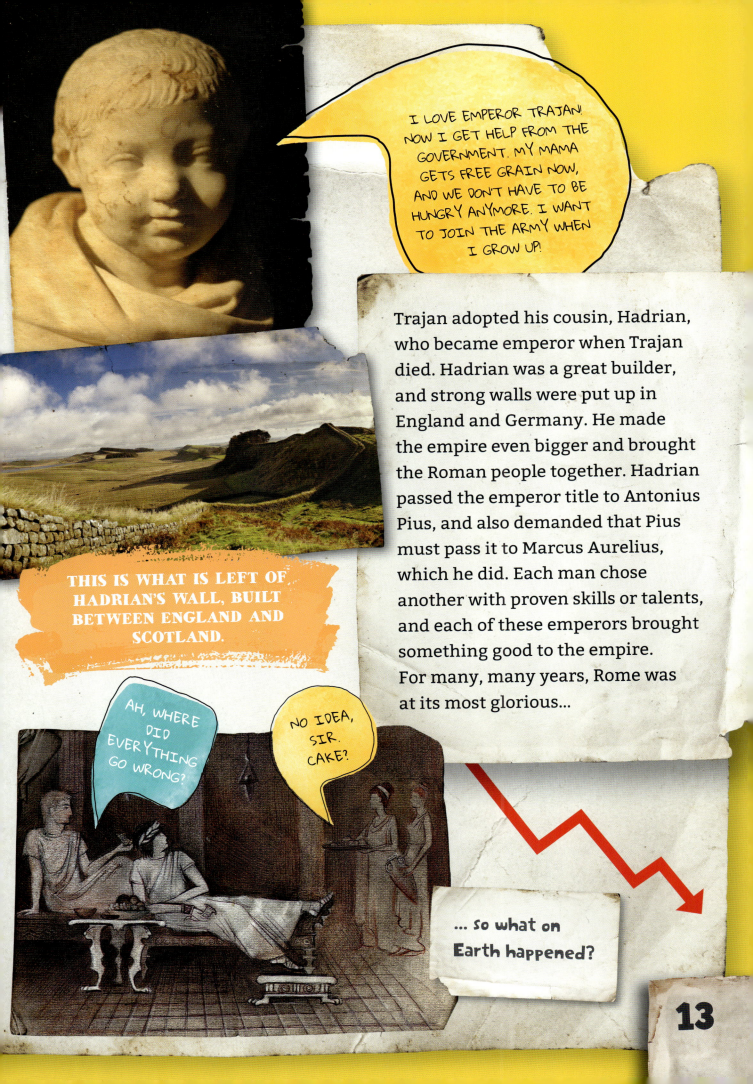

I LOVE EMPEROR TRAJAN! NOW I GET HELP FROM THE GOVERNMENT. MY MAMA GETS FREE GRAIN NOW, AND WE DON'T HAVE TO BE HUNGRY ANYMORE. I WANT TO JOIN THE ARMY WHEN I GROW UP!

Trajan adopted his cousin, Hadrian, who became emperor when Trajan died. Hadrian was a great builder, and strong walls were put up in England and Germany. He made the empire even bigger and brought the Roman people together. Hadrian passed the emperor title to Antonius Pius, and also demanded that Pius must pass it to Marcus Aurelius, which he did. Each man chose another with proven skills or talents, and each of these emperors brought something good to the empire. For many, many years, Rome was at its most glorious...

THIS IS WHAT IS LEFT OF HADRIAN'S WALL, BUILT BETWEEN ENGLAND AND SCOTLAND.

AH, WHERE DID EVERYTHING GO WRONG?

NO IDEA, SIR. CAKE?

... so what on Earth happened?

CIVIL WAR

GO ON, MY SON

Some say the beginning of the end started with Marcus Aurelius' son, Commodus. Marcus Aurelius did something different to the other 'Five Good Emperors' – he named his own son as **HEIR**.

HEY! I'M THE EMPEROR NOW! WOO-HOO! I DON'T KNOW WHY EVERYONE IS SAYING I'M TOO RICH AND NOT SERIOUS ENOUGH. WHAT? THIS? THIS IS MY LION HAT. IT'S MADE FROM A REAL LION, SO YOU KNOW IT'S GOOD.

Commodus was more like Caligula and Nero, and liked to live a rich life. He was assassinated by his own ministers and Rome broke out into **CIVIL WAR**. Rome then had five emperors in just one year.

COMMODUS

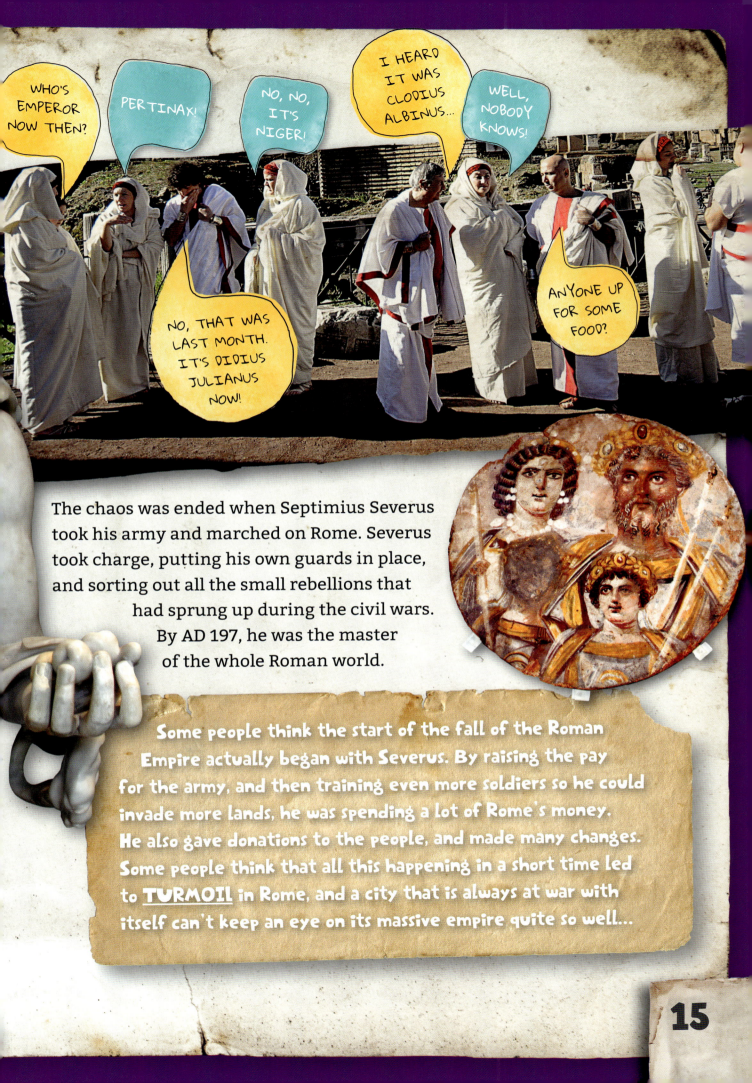

The chaos was ended when Septimius Severus took his army and marched on Rome. Severus took charge, putting his own guards in place, and sorting out all the small rebellions that had sprung up during the civil wars. By AD 197, he was the master of the whole Roman world.

Some people think the start of the fall of the Roman Empire actually began with Severus. By raising the pay for the army, and then training even more soldiers so he could invade more lands, he was spending a lot of Rome's money. He also gave donations to the people, and made many changes. Some people think that all this happening in a short time led to TURMOIL in Rome, and a city that is always at war with itself can't keep an eye on its massive empire quite so well...

THE CRISIS OF THE THIRD CENTURY

Gallic Empire
Roman Empire
Palmyrene Empire

N   0   500 km
     0   300 miles

IT'S TIME TO BREAK UP

It was AD 235 to AD 284. With all the chaos of the last few hundred years, things were starting to fall apart. The Empire split into three parts. A man named Postumus created the Gallic Empire (shown in green on the map). In AD 270, a queen called Zenobia took over the Palmyrene Empire (shown in yellow on the map). What was left was controlled by Rome.

QUEEN ZENOBIA

It may seem like this was a rebellion, but both Postumus and Zenobia said that they were actually helping Rome. The three parts of the empire were able to work together – although Postumus and Zenobia were definitely trying to get more power for themselves too. They got away with it because the Roman emperors were too busy fighting between themselves to do anything about it... until Aurelian turned up...

AURELIAN

OI! YOU CAN'T SPLIT UP MY EMPIRE LIKE THIS! ARREST THAT CHEEKY QUEEN - I DON'T CARE IF THIS IS FOR THE BEST! I WANT TO BE EMPEROR OF EVERYTHING!

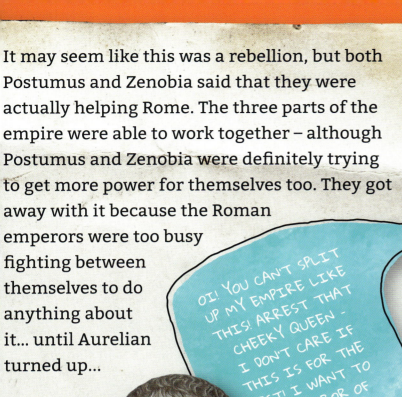

WELL, WHAT DO YOU THINK?

DIOCLETIAN

245 à 313 après J.C.
DIOCLÉTIEN
EMPEREUR de 284 à 313 ap. J.C.

Finally, emperor **Diocletian** took over and made an unusual decision. He realised the empire was too big for one man to rule and so shared power with his friend Maximian. Diocletian was a politician and Maximian was a soldier. Maximian took control of the West, and **Diocletian** looked after the East.

WAIT, WHAT?
TO PRONOUNCE THESE WORDS, SAY:

DIOCLETIAN = DIE-OH-CLEE-SHUN
MAXIMIAN = MAX-IMMI-AN

EAST MEETS WEST

The Roman Empire was now divided in a way it would never recover from. Diocletian split the empire further into four parts. Each part was ruled by a different leader.

North Sea

BRITANNIAE

BRITAIN

Rhine R.

GERMANIC PEOPLES

Trier ★

Tours

GALLIAE

ATLANTIC OCEAN

Rhône R.

A L P S

★ Milan

Ravenna

VIENNENSIS

ITALIA

Corsica

Rome

SPAIN

Sardinia

HISPANIAE

Hippo

Carthage

AFRICA

M

SEE ALL THAT GREEN, RIGHT THERE? GO ON. POINT TO IT. IT'S ALL MINE! I'M IN CHARGE AROUND THESE PARTS AND THAT'S JUST FINE BY ME. CAN YOU IMAGINE TRYING TO THINK ABOUT THIS WHOLE MAP? IT WOULD BE ENOUGH TO DRIVE YOU CRAZY... YOU'D END UP MAKING YOUR HORSE A CONSUL OR SOMETHING! HOW RIDICULOUS!

Diocletian and Maximian's idea to split the empire into four was working well. Each emperor could look after a smaller area of **TERRITORY** and keep everything running smoothly. Diocletian was the overall emperor, and Maximian was second to him. They were both known as **Augustus**. Each then adopted a son who would rule the smaller parts of the empire. These adopted sons were known as **Caesars** and they would eventually become the new **Augustuses**.

Diocletian chose a commander, a man named Constantius. Maximian chose a soldier, Galerius. Each Caesar had to answer to his adopted father, the Augustus. When the time came for them to take over, they should have had a lot of practice being a ruler. Was this the idea that would save the Roman Empire?

District of Constantius as Caesar
District of Maximian as Augustus
District of Galerius as Caesar
District of Diocletian as Augustus
ITALIA Dioceses and boundary
★ District capitals

OSTROGOTHS

DACIA

Danube R.

BALKAN MTS.

Black Sea

MOESIAE THRACIA Byzantium

alonika Chalcedon ★Nicomedia

MACEDONIA Nicaea

ASIANA PONT

Caesar

Athens Tyana

Ephesus

Antioch MESOPOTA

Crete SYRIA

ranean Sea Cyprus ORIENS

PALESTINE

Bethlehem

Alexandria

ARABIA

HEY. I'M CONSTANTIUS. I'VE BEEN RULING OVER HERE IN THE EAST FOR A WHILE NOW. I'VE CHOSEN MY SON AS MY HEIR. AND I'VE NAMED HIM AFTER ME! BEING A CAESAR IS GREAT!

WAIT, WHAT?
TO PRONOUNCE
THESE WORDS, SAY:

CONSTANTIUS = CON-STAN-TEE-US

GALERIUS = GAL-AIR-EE-US

CAESAR = SEE-ZER

CONSTANTINE

ANOTHER NEW EMPIRE?

After the deaths of the four emperors, there was some disagreement over who should rule, and how. And by "some disagreement" we mean war and chaos. Again. But why? Well, after each Augustus died, the Caesars moved up and named their own Caesars. However, neither man named their own actual son as Caesar, and the sons weren't too happy about it. Constantius' son, Constantine, and Maximian's son, Maxentius, got themselves declared emperor by their own armies. Can you guess what happened next? I mean, we are talking about the Romans here. They don't settle disagreements over a nice cup of tea...

LET'S TALK ABOUT JESUS CHRIST

Constantine defeated every challenger for this throne and was made **SOLE** emperor in **AD** 324. But there was something different about this new emperor. He was a Christian. For many years, it had been illegal to be Christian in Rome, and now the emperor himself was one! Constantine built a new capital city, naming it Constantinople. He filled it with churches, and Christianity grew and grew, eventually becoming the main religion of the empire. The old pagan gods were slowly forgotten.

THERE IS BUT ONE EMPEROR - ME! THERE IS BUT ONE GOD, AND THAT IS MY GOD! NOW NAME EVERYTHING AFTER ME. THE ROMAN EMPIRE IS SAVED!

TEA!

IMPERIVM ROMANORVM

THIS IS WHAT THE ROMAN EMPIRE LOOKED LIKE WHEN CONSTANTINE WAS IN CHARGE.

THE GOTHS

If we go forwards a few years (and a few emperors), we arrive in AD 378. Rome was now a Christian city, and the empire was divided in two – Emperor Valens ruling the east and Emperor Valentinian the west. The Romans were still trying to conquer more land while continuing to fight with each other all the time. But now they had bigger problems...

WE'RE THE GOTHS AND WE'VE BEEN LIVING UP HERE IN THE COLD NORTH. WE'RE REALLY, REALLY TOUGH. WE'VE NOTICED THAT YOU ROMANS DON'T SEEM AS TOUGH AS YOU USED TO BE... SO WE'VE BEEN HAVING BATTLES WITH YOU FOR A WHILE NOW. WE DON'T CARE IF YOU THINK WE'RE BARBARIANS... WE WANT YOUR EMPIRE! AAAAARGGHHHH!!

The Goths were headed for Constantinople. Valens, ruler of the Eastern Empire, took his forces to meet them but the Romans were confused and not ready. The Goths came down from the mountains like thunder, destroying the army and killing Valens. It was the worst Roman defeat for hundreds of years.

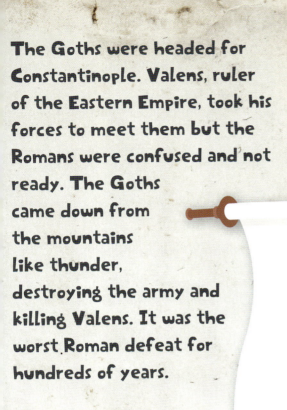

THIS IS THE BEGINNING OF THE END! I KNOW IT!

But those Romans knew how to hang on. The defeat was massive, but the next emperor was able to clean up the mess and make peace with the Goths. For a while...

WAIT, WHAT?
TO PRONOUNCE THESE WORDS, SAY

VALENS = VAL-ENZ

VALENTINIAN = VAL-EN-TIN-EE-AN

THE END OF THE WEST

(SPOILER ALERT)

Valens's grandsons, Arcadius and Honorius, took control around AD 393. They split the empire into two clear halves. The Eastern Empire was ruled by Arcadius and the Western Empire by Honorius. Honorius had real problems. The Goths, now split into two tribes (the Visigoths and the Ostrogoths), were attacking again and looking to invade. In AD 406, a tribe known as the Vandals from the **GERMANIC** area had crossed into the empire at Gaul and were heading for Hispania.

GOTHS TO THE LEFT OF ME, VANDALS TO THE RIGHT... HERE I AM, STUCK IN THE MIDDLE WITH... WELL, NOT AS MANY SOLDIERS AS I'D LIKE, AND BARBARIANS EVERYWHERE. AND THEY KEEP WINNING! I'M LOSING PARTS OF THE EMPIRE. THAT MEANS I'M ALSO LOSING SOLDIERS, AND MONEY. AT LEAST NO-ONE HAS INVADED ROME...

HONORIUS

WAIT, WHAT?
WHERE ARE THOSE PLACES?

GAUL = MODERN-DAY FRANCE

HISPANIA = MODERN-DAY SPAIN AND PORTUGAL

INVASION OF ROME

On the 24th of August, **AD** 410, the Visigoth King, Alaric, stormed Rome. For three days his troops **LOOTED AND PILLAGED** the city. It was the first time in 800 years that the city had fallen to a foreign enemy. Although it had been many years since Rome had been the capital of the Roman Empire, many historians agree that this was the first point in the true end of the Roman Empire in the west.

KING ALARIC

OH NO! ODOACER!

THE ABSOLUTE, REAL, ACTUAL END...

Some say that the last Roman emperor was Romulus Augustulus. Others (mostly people from the eastern empire at the time) say that he was a **PUPPET EMPEROR.** Romulus Augustulus was still a child when he became western emperor and his father Orestes was ruling until he was old enough. But by then, the Roman Empire was on its knees after many years of barbarian invasions and fighting among themselves. Rome was theirs for the taking...

HELLO, AUGUSTULUS. I AM ODOACER. I'VE DEFEATED YOUR TROOPS, I'VE EXECUTED ORESTES, AND I'M THE KING NOW. BUT LOOK. YOU'RE JUST A KID. IF YOU LET ME BE EMPEROR AND GIVE ME THAT SHINY CROWN, YOU CAN GO AND LIVE IN CAMPANIA. JUST DON'T COME BACK!

And that was it. With no Rome, no emperor, no Caesar and with the empire itself split and broken beyond all recognition, the ancient Romans were gone...

HEY! AREN'T I THE GOD OF LIGHTNING ANYMORE? DOES THAT MEAN I CAN PUT THESE LIGHTNING BOLTS DOWN?

The Eastern Empire would carry on as the Byzantine Empire for a long time. It became very wealthy. But they were not ancient Romans as we would know them. Their life of riches was very different from the togas, gladiators and Caesars of old.

WHERE DID EVERYONE ELSE GO? GUYS...?

WE DO THINGS A LITTLE DIFFERENTLY IN THE BYZANTINE EMPIRE. THEY EVEN LET US LADIES HAVE A SAY FROM TIME TO TIME! AMAZINGLY MODERN!

BYZANTINE EMPRESS THEODORA

27

WHAT REMAINS OF THE ANCIENTS?

Italy today is a modern place, with bustling cities and a thriving culture all of its own. But if you travel to modern-day Rome, you can still visit Roman temples and see the famous **MOSAICS**. Italy might be quite different now, but its history is all around us in the present day. Let's take a look at what the Romans left behind...

THE COLOSSEUM, WHERE GLADIATORS ONCE FOUGHT TO THE DEATH, STILL STANDS IN ROME. TOURISTS LIKE TO VISIT IT.

NEWSPAPERS

NEWS

WORLD ECONOMY BUSINESS TECHNOLOGIES SPORT ENTERTAINMENT MUSIC

The first newspaper was invented by Julius Caesar around 59 BC. It was called the Acta Diurna. It was carved in stone and displayed in a public place, to share important information with the people. Thankfully today, tablets are a little lighter...

MASS ENTERTAINMENT

The Romans loved to get together and have a good time. Theatre, gladiator fights and sporting events were a huge part of Roman life, and we still have a lot of their plays to see today.

GOVERNMENTS

THE ROMAN STYLE OF GOVERNMENT HELPED CREATE MANY OF THE GOVERNMENTS YOU SEE TODAY.

THE ROMAN FORUM

PLUMBING

ROADS

There is a saying: "All roads lead to Rome!" The Romans made really brilliant roads, building over 80,000 kilometres of them across the empire. Roman roads are known for being long-lasting and straight.

ROMAN AQUEDUCTS TOOK WATER INTO THE CITIES AND ROMAN SEWERS TOOK DIRTY WATER AND HUMAN SEWAGE AWAY. IN SOME PLACES, THE ROMAN SEWERS WERE SO GOOD THAT THEY LASTED WELL INTO THE 1800s!

GLOSSARY

ADOPTION
when someone is made part of the family by choice instead of being related to the family

ASSASSINATED
killed for reasons to do with power or religion

CIVIL WAR
a war between different groups in the same country

CONQUER
overcome or take control of something by force

CONSUL
someone who is hired to look after a city in a different country

CULTURE
the way of life and traditions of a group of people

DAUGHTERS-IN-LAW
daughters who are part of a family because of marriage, instead of being related to anyone

FAMINES
times when large numbers of people do not have enough food

GERMANIC
to do with the area of Europe around Germany

HEIR
someone who will get the objects, money and titles of a person who dies

ICONIC
when something is well known and a symbol of a place or time

LEGIONARIES

Roman soldiers

LOOTED AND PILLAGED

to have stolen from a place using force and violence

LYRE

an ancient musical instrument that was a bit like a guitar

MOSAICS

pictures or patterns that are created by putting together small pieces of stone, tile or glass

POLITICIAN

a person involved with politics and how the country is run

PROVINCE

an area that belongs to a certain country or empire

PUPPET EMPEROR

an emperor who has no real power and is controlled by someone else

REIGN

the time that a certain leader rules for

SEWAGE

water and waste material from humans

SOLE

the only one

TERRITORY

an area of land claimed and controlled by a country or empire

TURMOIL

a state of confusion, uncertainty or upset

INDEX

PHOTO CREDITS

All images are courtesy of Shutterstock.com, unless otherwise specified. With thanks to Getty Images, Thinkstock Photo and iStockphoto. Front Cover – Phant, ZaZa Studio, Andrey Yurlov, Merfin, spaxiax, AikStudio. 4&5 – Karl Allen Lugmayer, Razvan Stroie, Africa Studio, polkadot_photo, Hunter Bliss Images, Denis Zyatkov. 6&7 – Wilson Marcius, Natursports, Vuk Kostic, Luis Louro, delcarmat, Diego Delso. 8&9 – FooTToo, pcruciatti, Morphart Creation. 10&11 – PLRANG ART, Gilmanshin, Jackknife Barlow. 12&13 – Framo, Anagoria, riekephotos, Sara Winter, Yulliii. 14&15 – MZeta, José Luiz Bernardes Ribeiro, José Luiz Bernardes Ribeiro. 16&17 – Janusz Pienkowski, Creative Commons: Attribution-ShareAlike, Jebulon. 18&19 – Coppermine Photo Gallery, Rasiel Suarez, ashva. 20&21 – Regien Paassen, Natalia Paklina, Karl Spruner von Merz (Public domain). 22&23 – Kachalkina Veronika, Meilun. 24&25 – lynea, Augustine, La Cité de Dieu (Vol. I). Translation from the Latin by Raoul de Presles, Ludwig Thiersch (Public domain). 26&27 – delcarmat, Nejron Photo, Inspiring, Jean-Joseph Benjamin-Constant (Public domain). 28&29 – Leszek Bogdewicz, Meiqianbao, d13, Fotokvadrat, Kiev.Victor, steve estvanik. Paper – ZaZa Studio, Monica Butnaru, Ints Vikmanis, ZaZa Studio, Anton Watman. Speech Bubbles – Nataleana. Caption banner – Olga_C